WHAT IS THE BOOK OF RUTH?

Kids' Guides to God's Word Series

What Is the Book of Genesis?
What Is the Book of Exodus?
What Is the Book of Leviticus?
What Is the Book of Numbers?
What Is the Book of Deuteronomy?
What Is the Book of Joshua?
What Is the Book of Judges?
What Is the Book of Ruth?
What Is the Book of 1 Samuel?
What Is the Book of 2 Samuel?
What Is the Book of 1 Kings?
What Is the Book of 2 Kings?
What Are the Books of 1–2 Chronicles?
What Are the Books of Ezra & Nehemiah?
What Is the Book of Esther?
What Is the Book of Job?
What Is the Book of Psalms?
What Is the Book of Proverbs?
What Is the Book of Ecclesiastes?
What Are the Books of Song of Songs & Lamentations?
What Is the Book of Isaiah?
What Is the Book of Jeremiah?
What Is the Book of Ezekiel?
What Is the Book of Daniel?
What Are the Books of Hosea–Micah?
What Are the Books of Nahum–Malachi?
What Is the Gospel of Matthew?
What Is the Gospel of Mark?
What Is the Gospel of Luke?
What Is the Gospel of John?
What Is the Book of Acts?
What Is the Book of Romans?
What Is the Book of 1 Corinthians?
What Is the Book of 2 Corinthians?
What Is the Book of Galatians?
What Is the Book of Ephesians?
What Is the Book of Philippians?
What Are the Books of Colossians & Philemon?
What Are the Books of 1–2 Thessalonians?
What Are the Books of 1–2 Timothy & Titus?
What Is the Book of Hebrews?
What Is the Book of James?
What Are the Books of 1–2 Peter & Jude?
What Are the Books of 1-3 John?
What Is the Book of Revelation?

What Is the Book of

RUTH?

Michael Whitworth

ISBN 978-1-971767-03-1

Published by Start2Finish
Bend, Oregon 97702
start2finish.org

Printed in the United States of America

30 29 28 27 26 1 2 3 4 5

CONTENTS

INTRODUCTION

If I asked you to name the most important stories in the Bible, what would you say?

Most people would probably start with the big ones. Creation. Noah's ark. Moses and the ten plagues. David and Goliath. Daniel in the lions' den. Jesus walking on water. The resurrection.

Those are all amazing stories—dramatic, miraculous, larger than life. They have kings and prophets, battles and miracles, seas parting and giants falling. The kind of stories that make epic movies.

But here's something that might surprise you: one of the most important stories in the entire Bible has none of those things. No miracles. No battles. No kings (at least, not yet). No supernatural fireworks of any kind.

It's the story of two widows trying to survive. A young woman gleaning leftover grain in a field. A kind landowner who notices her. A late-night conversation on a threshing floor. A quiet wedding. A baby.

That's it. That's the whole story.

And yet this tiny book—just four short chapters tucked between Judges and 1 Samuel—turns out to be one of the most important stories ever told. Because that baby? His name was Obed. Obed grew up and had a son named Jesse. Jesse grew up and had a son named David—yes, *that* David, the giant-slayer, the king, the man after God's own heart. And if you trace the family line all the way down through history, you eventually get to a young woman named Mary, a carpenter named Joseph, and a baby born in a manger.

The story of Ruth is the backstory of Jesus.

But it's not just important because of how it ends. It's important because of what it teaches us along the way. In four short chapters, the book of Ruth tackles some of the biggest questions you'll ever face: What do you do when life falls apart? Is God really there when you can't see him? What does it mean to be truly loyal to someone? How does God work in ordinary, everyday moments? What does real love actually look like?

These aren't abstract theological questions. They're the questions you wrestle with when your parents are fighting, when your best friend moves away, when someone you love gets sick, when you feel like nobody understands you. The book of Ruth meets you right where you live.

Let me tell you what you're going to find in this book.

Chapter One is about what happens when everything falls apart. You'll meet a woman named Naomi whose life crumbles into pieces—she loses her husband, her sons, her home, and her hope. She's so devastated that she tells her friends to call her "Bitter" instead of her real name. But you'll also meet Ruth, her daughter-in-law, who refuses to abandon Naomi even when walking away would be the sensible thing to do. Ruth's famous words—"Where you go I will go, and where you stay I will stay"—aren't just poetry. They're a window into a kind of love that doesn't quit when things get hard.

Chapter Two is about coincidences that aren't really coincidences. Ruth goes out looking for food and "just happens" to end up in the field of a wealthy man named Boaz—who "just happens" to be a relative of Naomi's dead husband. What looks like random luck to Ruth is actually God working behind the scenes. This chapter will change how you think about the ordinary moments in your own life. Maybe that "random" friendship, that "accidental" conversation, that unexpected move to a new city—maybe none of it is as random as you thought.

Chapter Three is about taking bold risks. Naomi comes up with a plan to secure Ruth's future, and it involves Ruth doing something scary and vulnerable—approaching Boaz at night and essentially asking him to marry her. Everything could go wrong. She could be rejected, humiliated, or worse. But Ruth steps out in faith anyway. This chapter is for anyone who's ever had to do something brave, something that made your stomach flip, something that required trusting God with the outcome.

Chapter Four is about redemption. That's a big church word, but it basically means being rescued from a situation you couldn't escape on your own. Boaz steps up to rescue Ruth and Naomi—not because he has to, but because he wants to. He pays a price to make them part of his family. And in doing that, Boaz points us toward an even greater Redeemer who would one day pay an even greater price to rescue people who couldn't save themselves.

Along the way, you're going to learn some Hebrew words. Don't worry—I'll explain them as we go. But there's one word you need to know right from the start: *hesed*. It's pronounced "KHEH-sed," and it's one of the most important words in the entire Old Testament.

Hesed is hard to translate because no single English word captures everything it means. Translators have tried "kindness," "loyal love," "faithfulness," "mercy," and "steadfast love." But *hesed* is bigger than all of those words combined. It's the kind of love that sticks around when sticking around doesn't make sense. It's loyalty that goes way beyond what anyone could reasonably expect. It's showing up for someone even when you get nothing in return.

Ruth shows *hesed* to Naomi. Boaz shows *hesed* to Ruth. And behind it all, God is showing *hesed* to everyone—quietly, persistently, faithfully working to bring blessing out of brokenness.

The book of Ruth is really a book about *hesed*. And once you see it, you'll start noticing it everywhere—in your own life, in your relationships, and in the way God treats his people.

One more thing before we dive in.

This story takes place during one of the darkest times in Israel's history—the days of the judges, when everyone did whatever they wanted and things were falling apart. It would have been easy to think that God had forgotten his people, that nothing good could grow in such rocky soil.

But right in the middle of that darkness, God was writing a love story. A quiet one. An ordinary one. The kind that doesn't make headlines but changes everything.

Maybe that's where you are right now. Maybe your life feels dark. Maybe you're going through something hard, and it doesn't feel like God is doing anything at all.

If so, this book is for you. Because Ruth reminds us that God is always working, even when we can't see it. He's moving pieces into place. He's bringing the right people into our lives at the right moments. He's writing a story that's bigger than we can imagine.

All we have to do is trust him. And keep walking.

Ready? Let's go to Bethlehem.

1

WHEN EVERYTHING FALLS APART

If you've seen Pixar's *Inside Out*, you know the moment when everything goes wrong.

Riley is an eleven-year-old girl whose family just moved from Minnesota to San Francisco. She's lost her friends, her hockey team, her old house—basically everything that made her life feel normal. And inside her mind, things are even worse. Joy and Sadness have been accidentally sucked out of Headquarters, taking Riley's core memories with them. Fear, Anger, and Disgust are left trying to run the show, and they're doing a terrible job. Riley's personality islands start crumbling and falling into the Memory Dump. She stops feeling anything at all—just numb and empty.

From Riley's perspective, life is falling apart and there's nothing she can do about it. She feels alone. She feels like running away. She can't see any hope.

But here's what Riley doesn't know: deep inside her mind, Joy and Sadness are fighting their way back to Headquarters. They're riding the Train of Thought, navigating through Imagination Land, getting lost in Abstract Thought, even hitching a ride on a rocket with Riley's old imaginary friend Bing Bong. It's chaos, but they never stop trying to get home.

Riley can't see any of this. She has no idea that rescue is on the way. All she knows is that her world has collapsed and everything feels hopeless.

But the whole time—the *whole time*—something is happening beneath the surface. Joy and Sadness are working to save her, even when Riley can't feel them working. And in the end, when Sadness finally makes it back and Riley lets herself cry in her parents' arms, everything begins to heal.

I think about that movie whenever I read the first chapter of Ruth. Ruth 1 is a story about everything falling apart. A family loses their home. A woman loses her husband. Then she loses both of her sons. By the end of the chapter, Naomi—the main character—feels like her entire life has crumbled into dust. She even tells her friends to call her "Bitter" instead of her real name because that's exactly how she feels.

From the outside, Naomi's life looked like Riley's crumbling personality islands—nothing but collapse and ruin. But here's what Naomi couldn't see: underneath all that pain and loss, God was still at work. Like Joy and Sadness making their way through the maze of Riley's mind, God's plan was moving forward even when Naomi thought her world had completely fallen apart.

The first chapter of Ruth teaches us something really important: God doesn't abandon us when life gets hard. He might seem silent. He might seem far away. But he is always working beneath the surface, even when we can't see it or feel it. And often, he uses faithful friends—people who refuse to leave our side—to remind us that we're not alone.

If you've ever felt like your world was falling apart—maybe your parents got divorced, or someone you loved died, or your family had to move away from everything you knew—then this chapter is for you. Ruth 1 doesn't promise that life will always be easy. It doesn't pretend that pain isn't real. But it does show us that even in the darkest valleys, God is still God, and he still cares about you.

Let's dig in.

THE DARK DAYS OF THE JUDGES

The book of Ruth opens with a line that might seem boring at first glance: "In the days when the judges ruled." But to the original readers of this story, those words would have sent a shiver down their spines. It's like starting a scary movie with "It was a dark and stormy night." The audience immediately knows trouble is coming.

So what was so bad about the days when the judges ruled?

After Joshua led the Israelites into the Promised Land, the people were supposed to follow God and obey his commands. But they didn't. Instead, they fell into a terrible pattern that repeated over and over again: the people would rebel against God, God would allow their enemies to defeat them, the people would cry out for help, God would send a "judge" (which was more like a military hero than someone in a courtroom) to rescue them, and then everything would be okay for a while—until they rebelled again.

Each time this cycle repeated, things got a little worse. The judges became less heroic and more flawed. The people became more rebellious. By the end of the book of Judges, Israel was in complete chaos. The very last verse of Judges tells us, "In those days there was no king in Israel. Everyone did what was right in his own eyes" (Judges 21:25).

Think about what that means. Imagine if your school had no teachers, no principal, and no rules. Everyone just did whatever they wanted. Sounds fun for about five minutes, right? But pretty soon, chaos would break out. The bigger kids would bully the smaller ones. Nobody would learn anything. Lunch would be a disaster. That's basically what was happening in Israel during the time of the judges—except way worse.

The final chapters of Judges tell stories that are so dark and disturbing, they've probably never been taught in your Sunday school class. People doing horrible things to each other, even within their own families. It was one of the most violent and godless times in Israel's history.

And that's the setting for the book of Ruth. Right in the middle of all that darkness, this small story takes place. It's like finding a beautiful flower growing in a junkyard. The book of Ruth shows us that even in the worst of times, God is still working, and faithful people can still shine like lights in the darkness.

A FAMILY IN CRISIS

The story begins with a man named Elimelech, his wife Naomi, and their two sons, Mahlon and Chilion. They lived in a town called Bethlehem, which means "house of bread." Pretty ironic name for a place experiencing a famine, right? The "house of bread" had no bread.

We don't know exactly what caused the famine—maybe a drought, maybe a locust plague, maybe the result of enemy attacks. What we do know is that Elimelech had to make a decision: stay in Bethlehem and watch his family starve, or pack up and move somewhere with food. He chose to move. Specifically, he moved his family to Moab.

Now, if you know your Old Testament history, you might be raising an eyebrow right now. Moab? Really? That's where he decided to go?

Moab was not a good place for an Israelite family to settle. They worshiped a god named Chemosh who demanded child sacrifice. They had been enemies of Israel for generations. And according to God's law, Moabites weren't even allowed to join Israel's worship assembly because of how they had treated God's people in the past.

So why did Elimelech go there? Probably because Moab was close by and had food. Sometimes when you're desperate, you make decisions you wouldn't normally make. We're not told whether Elimelech's choice was right or wrong—the Bible doesn't say. What we do know is that the family went to Moab planning to stay "for a while." That "while" turned into ten years.

During that decade, some things happened. First, Elimelech died. Naomi was now a widow in a foreign land. Her two sons married local women—Moabite women named Orpah and Ruth. And then, tragically, both sons died too. We're not told how any of them died. The narrator doesn't seem interested in giving us those details. What matters is the result: Naomi was left alone, without her husband and without her sons, in a country that wasn't her home.

In the ancient world, this was about as bad as things could get for a woman. Women depended on men—fathers, husbands, or sons—for protection and provision. A widow with no sons had almost no options. She couldn't own property (at least, not in a way that would help her survive). She couldn't get a job in the modern sense. Her choices were basically: find a male relative to take care of you, beg for charity, or die.

Naomi was completely devastated. Everything she had built her life around was gone.

THE ROAD BACK HOME

Then Naomi heard some news: the famine in Bethlehem was over. God had "visited" his people—a special word in Hebrew that means God showed up to help. The rains had returned, the crops were growing, and there was bread in the house of bread again.

Naomi decided to go home. She had nothing left in Moab except painful memories. Maybe, just maybe, her relatives back in Bethlehem could help her survive.

Her two daughters-in-law, Orpah and Ruth, started walking with her. But somewhere along the road, Naomi stopped and turned to face them.

"Go back," she said. "Go back to your mothers' homes. May the Lord show you kindness, just like you showed kindness to my sons and to me. May the Lord help you find new husbands and new homes."

This was actually a pretty selfless thing for Naomi to say. She was basically telling these young women, "Don't waste your lives on me. I'm old. I can't give you new husbands. Go back to Moab where you might have a chance at a normal life."

Both women started crying. "No!" they said. "We'll go with you to your people."

But Naomi pushed back harder. "Why would you come with me?" she asked. "I'm too old to get married again. Even if I somehow had more sons tonight, would you wait around for twenty years until they were old enough to marry? No, my daughters. My life is too bitter. The Lord's hand has turned against me."

At this point, Orpah made a decision. She kissed Naomi goodbye and headed back to Moab. It was the sensible choice. It was the practical choice. Nobody would have blamed her for it. She was doing exactly what Naomi had told her to do.

But Ruth refused to leave.

WORDS THAT CHANGED EVERYTHING

What Ruth said next is one of the most famous speeches in the entire Bible. People recite these words at weddings all the time (even though the speech is actually from a daughter-in-law to her mother-in-law, not from a bride to a groom). Here's what Ruth said: "Don't urge me to leave you or to turn back from you. Where you go I will go, and where you stay I will stay. Your people will be my people and your God my God. Where you die I will die, and there I will be buried. May the Lord deal with me, be it ever so severely, if even death separates you and me."

Read those words again slowly. Think about what Ruth was promising. She was promising to leave her homeland forever. She was promising to abandon her family, her culture, her language, and her gods. She was promising to follow Naomi into a future that looked absolutely hopeless—two widows with no money, no men to protect them, and no real prospects for survival.

Why would anyone make that kind of promise?

The answer is found in a Hebrew word that shows up throughout the book of Ruth: *hesed*. It's pronounced "KHEH-sed," and it's one of the most important words in the whole Old Testament. Translators have tried to capture its meaning with words like "kindness," "lovingkindness," "loyalty," "faithful love," or "mercy." But *hesed* is bigger than any one English word.

Hesed is the kind of love that sticks around when sticking around doesn't make sense. It's the friend who stays by your side when everyone else walks away. It's doing good to someone even when you get nothing in return. It's loyalty that goes beyond what anyone could reasonably expect.

Ruth showed *hesed* to Naomi. She didn't have to. There was no law requiring her to follow her mother-in-law. Naomi had released her from any obligation. But Ruth's love wasn't based on obligation—it was based on commitment. She had decided that Naomi's God would be her God, and that meant she would love Naomi the way God loves his people: with a fierce, stubborn, never-give-up kind of love.

When Naomi saw that Ruth was absolutely determined to come with her, she stopped arguing. Together, the two women walked toward Bethlehem.

A BITTER HOMECOMING

When Naomi and Ruth arrived in Bethlehem, the whole town started buzzing. "Can this really be Naomi?" the women asked.

Remember, Naomi had been gone for over ten years. When she left, she was a married woman with a husband and two sons. Now she was returning as a broken, grief-stricken widow with nothing but a foreign daughter-in-law at her side.

Naomi's response was heartbreaking: "Don't call me Naomi," she said. "Call me Mara, because the Almighty has made my life very bitter. I went away full, but the Lord has brought me back empty. Why call me Naomi? The Lord has afflicted me; the Almighty has brought misfortune upon me."

Naomi's name meant "pleasant" or "sweet." But she didn't feel pleasant anymore. She felt bitter—so bitter that she wanted a new name to match her new reality. "Mara" means "bitter."

Notice something important here: Naomi blamed God for her suffering. She said, "The Lord has afflicted me. The Almighty has brought misfortune upon me." She wasn't being polite about it. She was angry. She was hurt. She felt like God had turned against her.

Was Naomi right? Was God really out to get her?

No. But Naomi couldn't see that yet. Her grief was so overwhelming that she couldn't see past it. She couldn't see that God had ended the famine and made it possible for her to come home. She couldn't see that God had given her Ruth—a daughter-in-law who loved her with extraordinary *hesed*. She couldn't see that God was already putting pieces in place to restore her life in ways she couldn't imagine.

Here's something really sad: when Naomi said "I went away full, but the Lord has brought me back empty," she was standing right next to Ruth. Ruth was literally there, and Naomi called herself "empty." It's like Ruth didn't even count.

That's what grief can do to us. When we're in deep pain, we sometimes can't see the blessings that are right in front of us. We focus so much on what we've lost that we can't see what we still have.

But the narrator of this story sees what Naomi can't see. And he gives us a little clue at the very end of chapter one: "So Naomi returned from Moab accompanied by Ruth the Moabite, her daughter-in-law, arriving in Bethlehem as the barley harvest was beginning."

Did you catch that? The barley harvest was beginning. That means there was food. That means there was hope. The famine was over. New life was springing up from the ground. And as we'll see in the chapters to come, Ruth's presence in Bethlehem—the Moabite woman who refused to leave Naomi's side—would turn out to be one of the greatest blessings in all of Israel's history.

Naomi couldn't see it yet. But God was working beneath the surface.

WHAT THIS MEANS FOR US

So what does any of this have to do with your life? You're probably not a widow in ancient Israel. You've probably never experienced a famine. But I'm guessing you know what it feels like when life falls apart.

Maybe your parents announced they're getting divorced, and suddenly your whole world got turned upside down. Maybe someone you loved—a grandparent, a friend, even a pet—died, and you're still trying to figure out how to live without them. Maybe your family had to move to a new city, and you had to leave behind all your friends and start over at a school where you don't know anyone. Maybe you're dealing with something at home that you can't talk about—something scary or painful or confusing—and you feel completely alone.

If any of that sounds familiar, then Ruth chapter one has some important things to say to you.

First, it's okay to be sad. Naomi didn't pretend everything was fine. She was honest about her pain. She called herself "bitter" because she felt bitter. The Bible doesn't tell us to fake happiness when our hearts are breaking. God can handle our honest emotions—even our anger, even our confusion, even our complaints. If you're hurting, it's okay to admit it.

Second, God is still at work even when you can't see him. Naomi thought God had abandoned her. She thought God was against her. But she was wrong. God was working the whole time—ending the famine, bringing her home, providing Ruth to care for her. Sometimes the hardest part of suffering is that we can't see what God is doing. We have to trust that he's there, even when it doesn't feel like it. The book of Ruth shows us that God's silence doesn't mean God's absence.

Third, we need faithful friends. Ruth's *hesed*—her stubborn, loyal love—was one of the main ways God took care of Naomi. Naomi needed someone who would stick with her through the hard times. And Ruth needed someone to be faithful to. God designed us to need each other. When you're going through something difficult, look for the "Ruths" in your life—the people who refuse to leave your side. And when someone you know is struggling, be a Ruth to them. Don't walk away. Don't give up. Stay.

Fourth, the end of the story matters. Chapter one of Ruth is pretty depressing. Death, loss, grief, bitterness—it's a rough way to start a book. But chapter one isn't the whole story. If you stopped reading here, you'd miss everything that comes next: the surprising romance, the dramatic rescue, and the incredible ending that connects this little story to God's plan to save the whole world. When you're in the middle of a hard chapter of your own life, remember that God isn't finished writing your story yet.

TALKING POINTS

Here are some things to think about and discuss:

1. **Naomi told Ruth to go back to Moab, but Ruth refused.** Think about a time when someone you loved was pushing you away. Why do people sometimes push others away when they're hurting? How should we respond when that happens?

2. **Ruth made a huge decision to leave everything she knew and follow Naomi.** Have you ever had to make a really hard choice because you knew it was the right thing to do? What made it hard? What helped you follow through?

3. **Naomi couldn't see God's blessings because she was so focused on her pain.** Can you think of a time when you were so upset about something that you couldn't see the good things in your life? What helped you eventually see things more clearly?

4. **The book of Ruth shows us *hesed*—faithful, loyal love that doesn't give up.** Who in your life has shown you that kind of love? How can you show *hesed* to someone else this week?

5. **Naomi felt like God was against her, but he wasn't.** Why do you think it's so hard to trust God when life gets difficult? What helps you remember that God is good even when circumstances are hard?

The barley harvest was beginning. That single detail at the end of chapter one is like a tiny ray of light breaking through storm clouds. The worst wasn't over for Naomi—not yet. She would still have dark days ahead. But the harvest was starting. New life was coming.

Hold on to that. Whatever you're going through right now, the harvest is coming. God is working beneath the surface, even when you can't see it. And he often works through faithful friends who refuse to walk away.

Don't give up. The best part of the story is still ahead.

2

NO SUCH THING AS LUCK

If you've seen *Kung Fu Panda*, you probably remember the moment when Po becomes the Dragon Warrior. He wasn't supposed to be there. He was just a clumsy panda who sold noodles with his dad—not exactly warrior material. But when Master Oogway was about to choose the legendary Dragon Warrior from among the Furious Five, Po desperately wanted to see what was happening. He couldn't get through the crowd. He couldn't climb the wall. In desperation, he strapped himself to a chair full of fireworks and launched into the sky.

He crash-landed right in front of Master Oogway—at the exact moment the old turtle was pointing to select the Dragon Warrior. And just like that, the bumbling noodle chef became the chosen one.

Accident? Coincidence? That's what everyone thought. Tigress, Viper, Crane, Mantis, Monkey—they were all furious. Shifu tried everything to get rid of Po, certain that a mistake had been made. But Master Oogway saw things differently. When Shifu complained that Po's selection was an accident, the wise turtle simply said, "There are no accidents."

That line stuck with me long after the movie ended. *There are no accidents.* What looked like random chaos—a fireworks chair, a crash landing, a pointed finger—was actually something more. Oogway could see what everyone else couldn't: Po was exactly where he was supposed to be.

Here's the thing about our lives: we look at events from ground level. We see a series of random moments bumping into each other like billiard balls on a pool table. We see luck, chance, coincidence. But God sees things from a different angle. He sees the whole picture—past, present, and future—all at once. And what looks like accident to us is often design to him.

Maybe you've experienced this yourself. You sit down at a random lunch table on the first day of school, and the kid next to you becomes your best friend for the next decade. Your family moves to a new city because of your parent's job, and it turns out to be the place where you discover what you're passionate about. You miss your bus and end up walking home a different route, where you find a lost dog and return it to a neighbor who ends up becoming like a grandparent to you.

In the moment, these things feel random. Looking back, they feel like something else entirely.

The second chapter of Ruth is all about those moments that look like coincidences but aren't. Ruth "just happens" to end up in the field of a man named Boaz. Boaz "just happens" to show up at the field that very day. He "just happens" to notice Ruth among all the other workers. And Boaz "just happens" to be a relative of Naomi's dead husband—one of the few people in all of Israel who could actually rescue these two widows from poverty and despair.

Luck? Coincidence? The narrator of Ruth wants us to smile knowingly. We serve a God who doesn't do "coincidences." What looks like chance to us is actually providence—God's mysterious hand guiding events toward his good purposes, even when we can't see it happening.

If chapter one of Ruth taught us that God doesn't abandon us when life falls apart, chapter two teaches us something equally important: God is always working, even when we can't see him. He's moving pieces into place. He's opening doors we didn't know existed. He's bringing the right people into our lives at exactly the right moments.

And often, he does it in ways that look completely ordinary.

A MAN NAMED BOAZ

Before the action of chapter two begins, the narrator introduces us to a new character. His name is Boaz, and he's about to become very important to this story.

The Hebrew text describes Boaz with a phrase that can be translated several different ways. Some Bibles say he was "a man of standing" or "a prominent man." Others say he was "a mighty man of valor" or "a worthy man." The phrase suggests someone who is wealthy, respected, influential, and morally upright. Boaz wasn't just rich; he was the kind of person everyone in town looked up to. He was a pillar of the Bethlehem community.

We also learn something crucial: Boaz was related to Elimelech, Naomi's dead husband. He was part of the same clan, the same extended family. This detail might seem minor, but it's actually huge. In ancient Israel, family members had special responsibilities to take care of each other. If a relative fell on hard times, other family members were supposed to step in and help. Boaz wasn't just any wealthy landowner—he was family.

The narrator tells us all this before the story even gets going. It's like watching a movie where the camera zooms in on a character's face and dramatic music plays, signaling to the audience: "Pay attention to this person. They're going to matter." The original readers of Ruth would have immediately understood: if Boaz is family, then maybe—just maybe—there's hope for Naomi and Ruth after all.

But here's the thing: Ruth doesn't know any of this yet. She has no idea who Boaz is. She doesn't know he's related to Naomi. She doesn't know he's wealthy and influential. All she knows is that she and her mother-in-law are desperately poor, and somebody needs to find food.

So Ruth takes the initiative.

RUTH GETS TO WORK

"Let me go to the fields," Ruth says to Naomi, "and pick up the leftover grain behind anyone in whose eyes I find favor."

This might sound strange to us today, but Ruth was talking about an ancient practice called "gleaning." In Israel, God had commanded landowners not to harvest every last bit of grain from their fields. They were supposed to leave the edges unharvested and not go back to pick up any stalks that the workers dropped. Why? So that poor people, widows, orphans, and foreigners could follow behind the harvesters and gather the leftovers for themselves.

It was basically an ancient welfare system—but one that required the poor to actually work for their food. You didn't just show up and receive a handout. You had to walk behind the harvesters all day in the hot sun, bending down over and over again to pick up dropped stalks of grain. It was backbreaking work, and it didn't pay much. On a good day, a gleaner might gather enough grain to make bread for a few days. It was survival-level labor.

And here's the really important part: gleaning could be dangerous, especially for a woman. The harvesters were mostly men, and not all of them were noble characters. A foreign woman working alone in the fields was vulnerable to harassment, abuse, or worse. Remember, this was during the time of the judges, when "everyone did what was right in his own eyes." Laws existed, but people didn't always follow them.

Ruth knew all of this. She knew the risks. But she also knew that she and Naomi needed food, and she wasn't about to sit around waiting for someone else to solve their problems. She asked Naomi's permission, got a simple "Go ahead, my daughter" in response, and headed out to find a field.

And here's where the "coincidence" comes in.

THE "COINCIDENCE" THAT CHANGED EVERYTHING

The narrator tells us that Ruth "found herself working in a field belonging to Boaz" (Ruth 2:3). Some translations say she ended up there "as it turned out" or even—and I love this—"as luck would have it."

But the original Hebrew is even more interesting. The phrase literally means something like "her chance chanced upon" the field of Boaz. It's an unusual construction, and the narrator is being a little playful here. He's winking at the audience. From Ruth's perspective, she randomly stumbled onto this particular field. She had no idea whose property it was. She just picked a spot and started working.

But we, the readers, already know something Ruth doesn't: this field belongs to Boaz, the wealthy relative who might be able to help them. What looked like random chance to Ruth was actually God guiding her steps.

This is one of the most important lessons in the entire book of Ruth. God often works through what appears to be ordinary, everyday events. There are no angels appearing in this story. No voices from heaven. No miraculous signs. Just a young woman walking into a field and starting to work—and "happening" to end up in exactly the right place.

God's providence doesn't always look dramatic. Sometimes it looks like a series of small decisions and apparent coincidences that only make sense when you look back later. Ruth had no idea that her choice of fields that morning would change her entire life. But God knew.

BOAZ NOTICES RUTH

Later that same day, Boaz arrived at his field to check on the harvest. The first thing we learn about him is how he greeted his workers: "The Lord be with you!" And they responded, "The Lord bless you!"

This little exchange tells us a lot about Boaz. He wasn't one of those bosses who treats his employees like dirt. He cared about his workers and wasn't embarrassed to invoke God's blessing on them right there in the middle of the workday. Boaz was a man whose faith showed up in ordinary moments.

When Boaz noticed Ruth among the other workers, he asked his foreman about her. "Who does that young woman belong to?" In that culture, the question wasn't offensive—it was a way of asking about her family connections. "Whose daughter is she? Whose wife?"

The foreman's answer is revealing: "She is the Moabite who came back from Moab with Naomi. She said, 'Please let me glean and gather among the sheaves behind the harvesters.' She came into the field and has remained here from morning till now, except for a short rest in the shelter."

Notice what the foreman emphasizes. First, Ruth is "the Moabite"—a foreigner, an outsider. Second, she was polite enough to ask permission before gleaning. Third, she had been working incredibly hard all day, barely taking any breaks. Even though she was a stranger, her character was already making an impression.

Boaz didn't ignore Ruth or treat her with suspicion because she was from Moab. Instead, he walked over and spoke to her directly. What he said next must have shocked her.

EXTRAORDINARY KINDNESS

"My daughter, listen to me," Boaz said. "Don't go and glean in another field and don't go away from here. Stay here with the women who work for me. Watch the field where the men are harvesting, and follow along after the women. I have told the men not to lay a hand on you. And whenever you are thirsty, go and get a drink from the water jars the men have filled."

Put yourself in Ruth's sandals for a moment. She's a foreigner. A widow. A nobody. She showed up that morning hoping to gather enough dropped grain to survive another few days. And now the wealthy owner of the field is personally inviting her to stay, promising her protection, and offering her free access to the workers' water supply.

This was way beyond what the gleaning laws required. Boaz wasn't just following the rules—he was going above and beyond them. He was showing *hesed*, that beautiful Hebrew word we talked about in chapter one. *Hesed* is loyal love, faithful kindness, going the extra mile for someone even when you don't have to.

Ruth was so overwhelmed that she fell on her face before him. "Why have I found such favor in your eyes," she asked, "that you notice me—a foreigner?" Ruth was basically saying, "I'm a nobody. I don't belong here. Why are you being so kind to me?"

Boaz's answer reveals that he already knew her story: "I've been told all about what you have done for your mother-in-law since the death of your husband—how you left your father and mother and your homeland and came to live with a people you did not know before."

Word had gotten around Bethlehem. People were talking about the Moabite girl who had refused to abandon her mother-in-law. They knew about her pledge to follow Naomi, to adopt Israel as her people and Israel's God as her God. Ruth's *hesed* to Naomi had not gone unnoticed.

Then Boaz said something beautiful: "May the Lord repay you for what you have done. May you be richly rewarded by the Lord, the God of Israel, under whose wings you have come to take refuge."

The image of God's "wings" is powerful. It pictures a mother bird sheltering her chicks from danger, spreading her wings over them to keep them safe and warm. Boaz recognized that Ruth had made a courageous choice to leave everything familiar and seek shelter under the protection of Israel's God. He was praying that God would reward her for that faith.

What Boaz didn't realize—not yet, anyway—was that God was about to use *him* to answer that very prayer.

MORE THAN SHE EXPECTED

Boaz's kindness didn't stop with words. At lunchtime, he invited Ruth to eat with him and his workers. "Come over here," he said. "Have some bread and dip it in the wine vinegar." When she sat down with the harvesters, Boaz personally handed her roasted grain—so much that she ate her fill and still had leftovers.

Then, after lunch, Boaz quietly gave orders to his workers: "Let her gather among the sheaves and don't reprimand her. Even pull out some stalks for her from the bundles and leave them for her to pick up, and don't rebuke her."

This was unheard of. Normally, gleaners could only pick up what was accidentally dropped. They weren't allowed to gather among the sheaves—the bundles of grain that the workers had already tied together. But Boaz told his men to let Ruth glean from the best stuff. He even told them to deliberately drop extra grain for her to find.

By the end of the day, Ruth had gathered about an ephah of barley—roughly thirty pounds of grain. To put that in perspective, a normal gleaner might gather a few pounds on a good day. Ruth had collected enough to feed herself and Naomi for weeks. It was an extraordinary amount, and it was only possible because of Boaz's extraordinary generosity.

When Ruth brought the grain home and showed Naomi what she had gathered, her mother-in-law's eyes went wide. "Where did you glean today?" Naomi asked. "Where did you work? Blessed be the man who took notice of you!"

When Ruth told her it was Boaz, something changed in Naomi. For the first time since returning to Bethlehem, we hear hope in her voice.

NAOMI'S HOPE REAWAKENS

"The Lord bless him!" Naomi exclaimed. "He has not stopped showing his kindness to the living and the dead."

This is a dramatic turnaround from the Naomi we saw at the end of chapter one—the bitter woman who told everyone to call her "Mara" because God had made her life miserable. Now, suddenly, she's praising God for his kindness. What happened?

Naomi saw the pile of grain. She heard that Ruth had been treated with honor and protection. And when she learned the man responsible was Boaz—a relative of her dead husband—the pieces started coming together. This wasn't random. This wasn't luck. God was at work.

"That man is our close relative," Naomi told Ruth. "He is one of our guardian-redeemers."

That word "guardian-redeemer" translates the Hebrew term *go'el*. It's a crucial concept in this story, so let me explain what it means.

In ancient Israel, family was everything. If a person fell on hard times—lost their land, fell into debt, or was left without children—it was the job of the nearest male relative to step in and set things right. This relative was called the *go'el*, the redeemer. He might buy back land that a family member had been forced to sell. He might pay off debts to free a relative from slavery. In some cases, he might even marry a widow to provide for her and carry on the family name.

When Naomi called Boaz "one of our guardian-redeemers," she was saying that Boaz had the right and the responsibility to help them—to redeem them from their desperate situation. The fact that Ruth had "happened" to end up in his field wasn't just good luck. It was the beginning of an answer to all their problems.

For the first time, Naomi could see God's hand at work. The same God she had accused of being against her was actually working for her good all along. She just couldn't see it until now.

WHAT THIS MEANS FOR US

So what does Ruth chapter two have to say to you?

First, God is working even when you can't see him. Ruth had no idea she was walking into Boaz's field that morning. Naomi had no idea that God was about to provide for them in such an incredible way. From their limited perspective, it all looked like random chance. But God was orchestrating events behind the scenes.

The same is true in your life. You might not be able to see what God is doing right now. Your circumstances might feel random or even cruel. But the book of Ruth reminds us that God is always working, even in the small details—guiding your steps, opening doors, bringing the right people into your life at the right time. Just because you can't see his hand doesn't mean it isn't there.

Second, faithfulness gets noticed. Ruth had no way of knowing that people in Bethlehem were talking about her. She didn't do *hesed* to Naomi in order to build a good reputation. She did it because it was the right thing to do, because she genuinely loved her mother-in-law, and because she had committed herself to the God of Israel. But her faithfulness didn't go unnoticed. Boaz heard about it. The whole town heard about it.

When you do the right thing—when you're kind to people who can't pay you back, when you stay loyal to friends who are going through hard times, when you work hard even when nobody seems to be watching—people notice. More importantly, God notices. Your faithfulness matters, even when you feel invisible.

Third, God often provides through ordinary means. There's nothing supernatural about what happened in Ruth 2. No angels. No miracles. Just a woman walking into a field, a man choosing to be generous, and a pile of grain at the end of the day. God's provision came through ordinary work, ordinary kindness, and ordinary human relationships.

Sometimes we pray for God to help us, and then we sit back and wait for something dramatic to happen. But often, God's provision comes through everyday opportunities. It comes through the job you find, the friend who helps you out, the teacher who believes in you. God can use ordinary means to accomplish extraordinary purposes.

Fourth, show *hesed* to others. Boaz didn't have to be so generous to Ruth. The law only required him to let her glean in his field—not to feed her lunch, not to protect her, not to tell his workers to drop extra grain for her. Boaz went way beyond what was required because he was a man of *hesed*. He saw someone in need and chose to help, even though it cost him something.

You probably have more opportunities to show *hesed* than you realize. There's a kid at school who eats lunch alone. There's a classmate who struggles with the subject you find easy. There's a neighbor who could use some help. *Hesed* doesn't have to be dramatic. Sometimes it's as simple as noticing someone and choosing to be kind.

Fifth, God cares about vulnerable people. Throughout the Bible, God shows special concern for widows, orphans, foreigners, and the poor. He commands his people to take care of those who can't take care of themselves. In Ruth 2, we see this principle in action. Boaz represents what God's people are supposed to look like—using their resources and influence to protect and provide for those in need.

This should challenge us to think about how we treat vulnerable people in our own world. Are we using what God has given us to help others, or are we keeping it all for ourselves?

TALKING POINTS

Here are some things to think about and discuss:

1. **Ruth's day started out looking ordinary, but it turned out to be life-changing.** Can you think of a time when something that seemed random or ordinary turned out to be really important? How does this change how you think about "coincidences"?

2. **Boaz went way beyond what was required to help Ruth.** What's the difference between doing the bare minimum for someone and showing them *hesed*? Can you think of someone who has gone "above and beyond" for you?

3. **Ruth's reputation preceded her—Boaz already knew about her faithfulness to Naomi.** How does it make you feel to know that people are watching how you act, even when you don't realize it? Does that motivate you or stress you out?

4. **Naomi's attitude changed dramatically when she heard about Boaz.** What caused that change? Have you ever had a moment when you suddenly realized God was working in a situation where you thought he was absent?

5. **Boaz prayed that God would reward Ruth—and then God used Boaz to answer that prayer.** Has God ever used you to answer someone else's prayer? How can we make ourselves available to be part of God's provision for others?

The chapter ends with Ruth settling into a routine. She kept working in Boaz's fields for the rest of the harvest season—about six or seven weeks total. By the end, she and Naomi had enough food stored up to last for months. Their immediate crisis was over.

But something was still missing. Ruth had food, but she didn't have a home of her own. She had protection, but she didn't have a husband. She had provision, but she didn't have a future.

The last verse of chapter two gives us a quiet reminder: "And she lived with her mother-in-law." That simple statement highlights what Ruth still lacked. She was living in Naomi's house, not her own. She was a widow, not a wife. The story isn't over yet.

Naomi had called Boaz a *go'el*—a redeemer. She had seen the possibility of rescue. But possibilities don't always become realities. Would Boaz step up? Would Ruth's future be secured? Or would this promising beginning lead nowhere?

Stay tuned. The story is about to get a lot more interesting.

3

THE BOLDEST MOVE

You know that moment in a movie when everything comes down to one scene? The hero has been through all kinds of obstacles, and now there's only one thing left to do—something scary, something risky, something that could either fix everything or ruin everything. Think about Simba in *The Lion King* when he finally decides to go back to Pride Rock and face Scar. Or Anna in *Frozen* making the choice to sacrifice herself for Elsa. Or even Hiccup in *How to Train Your Dragon* when he walks into that arena knowing everyone expects him to kill Toothless, but he's about to do something completely different.

Those moments make your stomach flip, don't they? You're watching and you want to yell at the screen, "Do it! Just do it!" But you also kind of want to cover your eyes because you're not sure what's going to happen next. The character is about to take a huge risk—and everything depends on how the other person responds.

Now imagine that moment wasn't in a movie. Imagine it was your real life.

Maybe you've experienced something like it. There's the kid at school you want to be friends with, but you've never actually talked to them. One day you finally work up the courage to walk over to their lunch table and ask if you can sit down. Your heart is pounding. Your palms are sweaty. What if they say no? What if they laugh? What if everyone at the table stares at you like you're weird?

Or maybe you've had to ask a teacher for help after class, and you were embarrassed because you didn't understand something everyone else seemed to get. Maybe you tried out for a team or auditioned for the school play, knowing that rejection was a real possibility. Maybe you had to apologize to a friend after a fight, even though you weren't sure they would forgive you.

Those moments take courage. Real courage. Not the kind of courage where you're fighting dragons or saving the world—but the quieter kind, where you have to be vulnerable, put yourself out there, and trust that the other person will respond with kindness instead of cruelty.

Ruth 3 is one of those moments.

Everything Ruth and Naomi have been working toward comes down to one risky, late-night encounter. Ruth has to do something bold—something that could be completely misunderstood, something that could ruin her reputation and destroy everything good that has happened so far. But if she doesn't take this risk, nothing will change. She and Naomi will remain poor widows with no future, no security, and no hope.

So Ruth takes the boldest step of her life. And what happens next will change everything—not just for her, but for the entire history of God's people.

This chapter teaches us something important: sometimes following God requires courage. It requires stepping out into the unknown, trusting that God is working even when we can't see how things will turn out. It requires being willing to take risks for the people we love.

Let's see what happens when Ruth decides to make her move.

NAOMI HAS A PLAN

Several weeks have passed since Ruth started gleaning in Boaz's fields. The barley harvest is over. The wheat harvest is over too. Ruth has been working hard, and thanks to Boaz's generosity, she and Naomi have plenty of food stored up. Their immediate crisis is solved.

But Naomi has been thinking. Yes, they have food—but food isn't everything. Ruth is still a young widow living with her mother-in-law. She doesn't have a husband. She doesn't have children. She doesn't have a home of her own. And what happens when Naomi dies? Ruth will be completely alone in a foreign country with no one to take care of her.

Naomi loves Ruth. Remember, back in chapter one, Naomi tried to send Ruth away because she thought Ruth would have a better life in Moab. That didn't work—Ruth refused to leave. But Naomi's concern for Ruth hasn't gone away. She wants Ruth to be secure, to be settled, to have a real home and a real future.

So Naomi comes up with a plan.

"My daughter," she says to Ruth, "should I not try to find a home for you, where you will be well provided for?"

The word Naomi uses for "home" means a place of rest,

security, and peace. It's the same word she used back in chapter one when she prayed that Ruth would find rest "in the home of another husband." Naomi knows that in their culture, the best way for Ruth to find that kind of security is through marriage.

And Naomi has a specific man in mind: Boaz. "Now Boaz, with whose women you have worked, is a relative of ours," Naomi reminds Ruth. "Tonight he will be winnowing barley on the threshing floor."

Here's where things get interesting—and a little unusual for us modern readers. Naomi doesn't tell Ruth to send Boaz a text, or to have a mutual friend set them up, or to ask him out for coffee. Instead, she gives Ruth a very specific—and very strange—set of instructions.

"Wash, put on perfume, and get dressed in your best clothes. Then go down to the threshing floor, but don't let him know you are there until he has finished eating and drinking. When he lies down, note the place where he is lying. Then go and uncover his feet and lie down. He will tell you what to do."

Okay, let's pause here. If you're thinking, *Wait, what? That sounds really weird*, you're not alone. What exactly is Naomi telling Ruth to do? And why would she tell her to do it this way?

UNDERSTANDING THE PLAN

First, let's talk about what's going on. Boaz has been winnowing grain at the threshing floor. Winnowing is the process of separating the grain from the chaff—the useless outer covering. Workers would toss the harvested grain into the air, and the wind would blow the light chaff away while the heavier grain fell back down. It was hard work, and it happened at the end of the harvest season.

The threshing floor was usually a flat, open area outside of town—often on a hilltop where the wind was strong. After a long day of work, the men would often sleep near the grain piles to protect them from thieves or animals. That's why Boaz would be spending the night there.

Naomi's instructions to Ruth have three parts:

First, get ready. "Wash, put on perfume, and get dressed in your best clothes." This wasn't just about looking nice—it was symbolic. Ruth had been wearing the dark clothing of a mourning widow ever since her husband Mahlon died. By washing, putting on perfume, and changing her clothes, Ruth was signaling that her period of mourning was over. She was ready to move on with her life. She was available for marriage.

Second, go to the threshing floor. Ruth was supposed to watch from a distance, wait until Boaz had eaten and drunk and fallen asleep, and then approach quietly without being seen.

Third, uncover his feet and lie down. This is the part that sounds strangest to us. What does it mean to "uncover his feet"? Some think the word "feet" is actually a polite way of referring to another body part (the Bible sometimes uses euphemisms like this). Others think it's more literal—Ruth was supposed to uncover Boaz's actual feet so that when he got cold in the night, he would wake up and discover her there.

Either way, the point is clear: Ruth was going to put herself in a vulnerable position, approach a man at night, and essentially ask him to marry her.

This was risky. Really risky. Here's why: The threshing floor had a reputation in ancient Israel as a place where inappropriate things sometimes happened. When workers finished their labor and celebrated with food and drink, things could get out of hand. For Ruth to go there alone at night—as a young, foreign woman—was dangerous. If anyone saw her, her reputation could be destroyed. People might assume the worst.

But Naomi knew something important: Boaz was a man of integrity. He wasn't the kind of person who would take advantage of Ruth. And Ruth wasn't going there for anything immoral—she was going to propose marriage. She was going to ask Boaz to be her *go'el*, her redeemer.

RUTH TAKES THE RISK

The text tells us simply: "I will do whatever you say," Ruth answered. And she went and did everything her mother-in-law told her to do.

Think about how much trust this required. Ruth trusted Naomi's judgment. She trusted that this plan—as strange as it seemed—was the right thing to do. And she trusted that Boaz would respond honorably.

That night, after Boaz had finished eating and drinking and was in good spirits, he went to lie down at the far end of the grain pile. Ruth approached quietly. Her heart must have been pounding. Every step brought her closer to a moment that could change everything—or ruin everything.

She uncovered his feet and lay down.

Sometime in the middle of the night—the text says it was around midnight—something startled Boaz awake. Maybe the cold air on his uncovered feet. Maybe a sound. He turned over, and suddenly he realized: there was a woman lying at his feet.

"Who are you?" he asked.

This is it. This is the moment everything hinges on. Ruth's response will determine what happens next.

"I am your servant Ruth," she said. "Spread the corner of your garment over me, since you are a guardian-redeemer of our family."

WHAT RUTH WAS REALLY ASKING

Ruth's words are loaded with meaning. Let's unpack them.

First, she calls herself Boaz's "servant." But the Hebrew word she uses is different from the word she used back in chapter two. The first word refers to a low-ranking servant with no rights. The second word—the one she uses here—can refer to a servant who might become a wife. Ruth is subtly raising her status. She's no longer just a gleaner in his fields. She's presenting herself as a potential bride.

Second, she asks Boaz to "spread the corner of your garment over me." This is a beautiful phrase with deep meaning. The Hebrew word for "corner" also means "wing." Remember what Boaz said to Ruth back in chapter two? "May you be richly rewarded by the Lord, the God of Israel, under whose wings you have come to take refuge."

Ruth is cleverly echoing his own words back to him. *You prayed that God would cover me with his wings. Now I'm asking you to cover me with yours. Be the answer to your own prayer.*

In that culture, spreading your garment over someone was a symbol of protection, provision, and marriage. The prophet

Ezekiel uses this same image when he describes God's covenant relationship with Israel: "I spread the corner of my garment over you and covered your naked body. I gave you my solemn oath and entered into a covenant with you, declares the Sovereign Lord, and you became mine" (Ezekiel 16:8).

Ruth is asking Boaz to marry her.

Third, she reminds him that he is a "guardian-redeemer"—a *go'el*. We talked about this word back in chapter two. The *go'el* was a close relative who had the responsibility to rescue family members who were in trouble. He could buy back land that a poor relative had been forced to sell. He could pay debts to free a relative from slavery. And in some cases, he could marry a widow to carry on the family name and provide for her future.

Ruth isn't just asking for romance. She's asking Boaz to step up and fulfill his family responsibility. She's asking him to rescue her and Naomi from their desperate situation.

And here's the really beautiful part: Ruth didn't have to do this. Naomi's plan was focused on finding security for Ruth—a husband, a home, a future. But when Ruth speaks to Boaz, she adds something that Naomi didn't mention. She brings up the *go'el* responsibility. She's not just thinking about herself—she's thinking about Naomi too. She wants Boaz to redeem them both.

Even in this risky, vulnerable moment, Ruth is showing *hesed*—that faithful, loyal love we keep seeing throughout this book.

BOAZ'S RESPONSE

How would Boaz respond? Would he be angry that Ruth had approached him this way? Would he be embarrassed? Would he reject her?

Listen to what he says: "The Lord bless you, my daughter. This kindness is greater than that which you showed earlier: You have not run after the younger men, whether rich or poor. And now, my daughter, don't be afraid. I will do for you all you ask. All the people of my town know that you are a woman of noble character."

Boaz is thrilled. He's not offended—he's honored. He calls Ruth's proposal an act of *hesed*, of kindness and loyalty. And he gives her one of the highest compliments in the entire Bible: he calls her a "woman of noble character" or "woman of valor."

Remember back in chapter two when the narrator introduced Boaz as a "man of standing" or "man of valor"? Now Ruth receives the same description. They're a perfect match. Two people of exceptional character, brought together by God's providence.

But there's a complication. "Although it is true that I am a guardian-redeemer of our family," Boaz says, "there is another who is more closely related than I."

Oh no. Another *go'el*. Someone who has a prior claim.

Boaz explains: "Stay here for the night, and in the morning if he wants to do his duty as your guardian-redeemer, good; let him redeem you. But if he is not willing, as surely as the Lord lives, I will do it."

Boaz is a man of integrity. Even though he clearly wants to marry Ruth, he won't cut corners. He won't ignore the proper legal process. If there's another relative with a closer claim, that man has to be given the first opportunity to act. Only if he refuses can Boaz step in.

But notice how Boaz ends his speech: "As surely as the Lord lives, I will do it." That's an oath. A solemn promise. Boaz is telling Ruth: *If there's any way I can make this happen, I will. Trust me.*

THE MORNING AFTER

Ruth stayed at the threshing floor until morning, but she got up early, before it was light enough for anyone to recognize her. Both she and Boaz wanted to protect her reputation. Even though nothing inappropriate had happened, people might gossip if they saw her leaving the threshing floor at dawn.

Before she left, Boaz gave her a gift: six measures of barley. We aren't exactly sure how much this was—somewhere between thirty and sixty pounds of grain. It was a generous amount, and it was meant as a sign. Boaz told Ruth, "Don't go back to your mother-in-law empty-handed."

That word "empty" is significant. Remember what Naomi said when she first returned to Bethlehem? "I went away full, but the Lord has brought me back empty." Naomi felt like she had lost everything. But now, bit by bit, her emptiness was being filled. Ruth came home with food. Ruth came home with hope. And Ruth came home with a promise.

When Naomi saw Ruth arrive with all that grain, she asked, "How did it go, my daughter?"

The Hebrew text actually says something a little different: "Who are you, my daughter?" It's the same question Boaz asked on the threshing floor. But Naomi wasn't confused about Ruth's identity. She was asking, "What's your status now? Are you still a widow, or are you engaged? How did things turn out?"

Ruth told her everything—about Boaz's response, about

his willingness to help, about the complication with the other *go'el*, and about his solemn oath to resolve everything.

Naomi's response shows how well she knew Boaz's character: "Wait, my daughter, until you find out what happens. For the man will not rest until the matter is settled today."

Naomi was confident. Boaz was a man of action. He wouldn't delay. He wouldn't procrastinate. He would take care of business—and he would do it immediately.

WHAT THIS MEANS FOR US

Ruth 3 is one of the most unusual chapters in the Bible. A late-night encounter on a threshing floor, an unconventional marriage proposal, and a lot of cultural details that seem strange to modern readers. But underneath all those ancient customs, there are truths that still speak to us today.

First, sometimes faith requires bold action. Ruth didn't just sit around waiting for something good to happen. She didn't expect God to drop a husband into her lap without any effort on her part. When Naomi presented a plan, Ruth acted. She took a risk. She put herself out there.

Following God isn't always passive. Yes, we need to trust in God's timing and God's provision. But sometimes God calls us to step out in faith, to take action, to be bold. Ruth's courage at the threshing floor reminds us that faith and action go hand in hand.

Second, character matters more than appearance. Boaz didn't fall for Ruth because she was beautiful (although she may have been). He was drawn to her character. He praised her *hesed*—her loyal love, her faithfulness, her commitment to

Naomi. He called her a "woman of noble character" because of how she lived, not how she looked.

In a world that's obsessed with appearances—with followers and likes and looking perfect online—the book of Ruth reminds us what really matters. Are you a person of integrity? Do you keep your promises? Do you show up for the people you love, even when it's hard? Those are the things that make someone truly attractive.

Third, good people do things the right way. Boaz could have taken advantage of Ruth that night. Instead, he protected her. He could have ignored the other *go'el* and just married Ruth without going through the proper channels. Instead, he committed to doing things the right way, even though it meant waiting and risking that someone else might marry her first.

Integrity means doing the right thing even when no one is watching. It means following the rules even when you could get away with breaking them. It means treating others with respect and honor, even in private moments when you could treat them however you wanted. Boaz and Ruth both demonstrated extraordinary integrity in a situation where they easily could have compromised.

Fourth, waiting is part of the journey. The chapter ends with Ruth and Naomi waiting. They've done everything they can do. Now they have to trust Boaz to handle the rest. Waiting is hard. We want to know how things will turn out. We want resolution. We want the story to be finished. But sometimes God asks us to wait—and to trust that he's working even when we can't see it.

Fifth, God works through ordinary people who take extraordinary steps. Ruth wasn't a queen or a prophet or a warrior. She was a poor foreign widow who decided to be bold for the sake of someone she loved. And God used her story to accomplish something incredible—something that would eventually lead to King David and, ultimately, to Jesus himself.

You don't have to be famous or powerful for God to use you. You just have to be willing. Willing to trust. Willing to act. Willing to take risks for the right reasons.

TALKING POINTS

Here are some things to think about and discuss:

1. **Ruth took a big risk by going to the threshing floor.** What's the biggest risk you've ever taken? How did it turn out? What did you learn from that experience?

2. **Naomi encouraged Ruth to be bold.** Who in your life encourages you to take steps of faith? How do they support you when you're nervous about trying something new?

3. **Boaz responded to Ruth's proposal with kindness and honor.** How do you respond when someone is vulnerable with you? Do you treat them with respect, or do you take advantage of their trust?

4. **Boaz called Ruth a "woman of noble character."** What character qualities do you most admire in other people? What qualities do you want people to see in you?

5. **The chapter ends with waiting.** What are you waiting for right now? How do you handle the uncertainty of not knowing how things will turn out?

The threshing floor scene is over. Ruth has made her move. Boaz has given his word. But there's still one more obstacle to overcome—that mysterious other *go'el* who has a prior claim.

Will he step up and marry Ruth? Or will he step aside and let Boaz take his place?

The answer comes in chapter four. And when it does, it will change everything.

4

THE BIGGER STORY

Have you ever been watching a movie or TV show and suddenly realized that everything you've been watching was connected to something much bigger than you expected?

Think about the Marvel movies. You might start by watching *Iron Man*—just a story about a genius billionaire who builds a super suit. Then you watch *Captain America* and *Thor*, each seeming like their own separate adventures. But then, suddenly, *The Avengers* happens, and you realize: "Wait—all these stories were connected the whole time! They were all building toward something bigger!"

Or think about a puzzle. When you first dump the pieces out of the box, they look like random shapes and colors that don't make any sense. You pick up one piece—maybe it's got a bit of blue sky and what looks like part of a tree branch. By itself, it doesn't mean much. But as you keep working, connecting piece after piece, suddenly you step back and see the whole picture. A castle on a mountainside. A sunset over the ocean. A family gathered around a table. The little pieces that seemed random weren't random at all—they were all part of something beautiful that you couldn't see until the end.

Ruth 4 is the moment when we finally see the whole picture.

For three chapters, we've been following the story of two widows trying to survive. Naomi lost her husband and both her sons. Ruth gave up everything to follow her mother-in-law to a foreign country. They scraped by on gleaned grain. Ruth took a bold risk at the threshing floor. Boaz promised to help—but there was another relative who had first claim.

If you've been paying attention, you've probably been asking: "How is this going to end? Will Boaz actually marry Ruth? Will Naomi ever stop feeling bitter? Will these two women finally find the security they've been searching for?"

Chapter four answers all those questions. But it does something even more surprising: it reveals that this little story about a Moabite widow and an Israelite farmer was never really a "little" story at all. It was always part of something much, much bigger.

You see, the book of Ruth ends with a genealogy—a family tree. And that family tree doesn't just tell us who Ruth's son grew up to be. It tells us that Ruth's great-grandson would be King David, the greatest king in Israel's history. And if you know your Bible, you know that David's family line eventually led to someone even greater: Jesus, the Son of God, the Savior of the world.

Ruth had no idea, when she was picking up leftover grain in Boaz's field, that she was playing a role in God's plan to save the entire human race. Naomi had no idea, when she was crying out in bitterness against God, that her story would be remembered for thousands of years as an example of God's faithfulness. Boaz had no idea, when he chose to redeem this Moabite widow, that he was becoming an ancestor of the Messiah.

They were just ordinary people, living ordinary lives, making faithful choices one day at a time. But God was weaving their stories into his cosmic plan of redemption.

And here's the amazing thing: God is doing the same thing with your story. You might feel like your life is small and insignificant—just another kid going to school, doing homework, trying to figure things out. But the God who worked through Ruth and Naomi and Boaz is the same God who is working in your life right now. Your story matters more than you know.

Let's see how Ruth's story ends—and how it points us to the greatest story ever told.

A MAN WITHOUT A NAME

Remember where we left off? Ruth had proposed to Boaz at the threshing floor, asking him to be her *go'el*—her guardian-redeemer. Boaz was thrilled. He wanted to marry Ruth. But there was a problem: another relative had a closer claim. According to the rules, that man had to be given the first chance to act as redeemer.

So Boaz didn't waste any time. Early the next morning—the very same day Ruth came home from the threshing floor—Boaz went to the town gate and sat down.

In ancient Israel, the town gate wasn't just where you entered and exited the city. It was like a combination of a courthouse, a city hall, and a community center. Important business was conducted there. Legal decisions were made there. If you had a case to settle, the gate was where you went.

Boaz sat down and waited. And sure enough, the other relative came walking by. What a "coincidence"! (But by now, we know there are no coincidences in this story, right?)

"Come over here, my friend, and sit down," Boaz called out.

Here's something interesting: the narrator never tells us this man's name. He's called in Hebrew basically the equivalent of "Mr. So-and-So" or "John Doe." Throughout the entire chapter, he remains anonymous.

Why would the narrator leave out his name? Because names mattered in ancient Israel. Having your name remembered was a big deal—it meant your legacy lived on. This man, as we're about to see, made a choice that prioritized protecting his own stuff over helping his family. And the result? He's forgotten. Nameless. Just another "So-and-So" who missed his chance to be part of something great.

Boaz, on the other hand, made the opposite choice. He gave generously, loved sacrificially, and as a result, his name is still remembered thousands of years later. There's a lesson there.

THE DEAL AT THE GATE

Boaz gathered ten elders of the town to serve as witnesses. Then he presented the situation to Mr. So-and-So: "Naomi, who has come back from Moab, is selling the piece of land that belonged to our relative Elimelech. I thought I should bring the matter to your attention and suggest that you buy it in the presence of these seated here. If you will redeem it, do so. But if you will not, tell me, so I will know. For no one has the right to do it except you, and I am next in line."

Wait a minute—Naomi has land? This is the first we're hearing about it!

Here's what was probably going on: When Elimelech left Bethlehem during the famine, he didn't sell his land. Maybe he couldn't find a buyer during a famine, or maybe he planned to come back eventually. Either way, Naomi still technically had a claim to that property. But as a widow with no sons, she couldn't farm it herself. Her only option was to sell it—but according to Israelite law, family land was supposed to stay in the family. A close relative (a *go'el*) could "redeem" the land by buying it and keeping it within the clan.

Mr. So-and-So heard "land for sale" and his eyes lit up. "I will redeem it," he said immediately.

Land was valuable. Land meant wealth, security, and something to pass on to your children. This looked like a great deal—help out a poor relative AND add to your own estate? Sign him up!

But then Boaz dropped the bombshell. "On the day you buy the land from Naomi, you also acquire Ruth the Moabite, the dead man's widow, in order to maintain the name of the dead with his property."

In other words: "The land comes with Ruth. If you redeem the property, you're also agreeing to marry her and provide an heir for Mahlon, her dead husband. That heir will inherit the land you're buying."

Suddenly, Mr. So-and-So's enthusiasm evaporated. "Then I cannot redeem it," he said quickly, "because I might endanger my own estate. You redeem it yourself. I cannot do it."

What changed? The math. If Mr. So-and-So bought the land AND married Ruth AND they had a son together, that son would inherit the land—not Mr. So-and-So's existing children. He would spend his money, time, and resources raising a child who would get the property he had paid for. From a purely financial perspective, it was a bad investment.

Mr. So-and-So was willing to help family as long as it benefited him. But costly sacrifice with no personal payoff? No thanks.

THE SANDAL CEREMONY

To make the transfer official, Mr. So-and-So took off his sandal and gave it to Boaz. This might seem strange to us, but it was a recognized legal custom in ancient Israel. The narrator even pauses to explain it: "Now in earlier times in Israel, for the redemption and transfer of property to become final, one party took off his sandal and gave it to the other. This was the method of legalizing transactions in Israel."

Taking off your sandal and handing it over was like signing a contract today. It made the agreement official and binding. With that simple act, Mr. So-and-So transferred his redemption rights to Boaz.

Then Boaz stood up and made his public declaration: "Today you are witnesses that I have bought from Naomi all the property of Elimelech, Kilion, and Mahlon. I have also acquired Ruth the Moabite, Mahlon's widow, as my wife, in order to maintain the name of the dead with his property, so that his name will not disappear from among his family or from his hometown. Today you are witnesses!"

Notice what Boaz emphasizes: preserving the name of the dead. He's not just doing this for himself. He's honoring Elimelech, Kilion, and Mahlon by making sure their family line continues. He's rescuing Naomi and Ruth from poverty and disgrace. He's putting their needs above his own financial interests.

This is *hesed* in action—that faithful, loyal, self-sacrificing love we've seen throughout the book of Ruth.

THE COMMUNITY'S BLESSING

The elders and all the people at the gate responded with a beautiful blessing: "We are witnesses. May the Lord make the woman who is coming into your home like Rachel and Leah, who together built up the family of Israel. May you have standing in Ephrathah and be famous in Bethlehem. Through the offspring the Lord gives you by this young woman, may your family be like that of Perez, whom Tamar bore to Judah."

This is a remarkable blessing. Rachel and Leah were the wives of Jacob—the mothers of the twelve tribes of Israel. To compare Ruth to them was to say, "May this Moabite woman become as important to Israel's future as the founding mothers of our nation."

And the reference to Perez is significant too. Perez was born to Tamar and Judah in a complicated and scandalous story. But despite the messy circumstances of his birth, Perez became an ancestor of David—and of Jesus. The blessing was prophetic: Ruth's family really would become like the family of Perez.

The community was celebrating Ruth's full acceptance into Israel. The foreign widow who had arrived in Bethlehem with nothing was now being blessed by the entire town. She was no longer "Ruth the Moabite" in a negative sense—she was one of them.

THE BIRTH OF OBED

The narrator moves quickly through the next part: "So Boaz took Ruth and she became his wife. When he made love to her, the Lord enabled her to conceive, and she gave birth to a son."

After all the tension and uncertainty, the resolution comes in just one verse. Boaz and Ruth got married. God blessed them with a child. Simple as that.

But don't miss the detail: "The Lord enabled her to conceive." Remember, Ruth had been married to Mahlon for ten years and never had children. She may have been unable to have children—which would have made her even more "worthless" in that culture's eyes. But God opened her womb. The same God who ended the famine, who guided Ruth to Boaz's field, who orchestrated every "coincidence" in this story—that God gave Ruth a son.

And now the focus shifts back to Naomi.

The women of Bethlehem—the same women who had greeted bitter Naomi when she first returned—now gathered around her with a very different message: "Praise be to the Lord, who this day has not left you without a guardian-redeemer. May he become famous throughout Israel! He will renew your life and sustain you in your old age. For your daughter-in-law, who loves you and who is better to you than seven sons, has given him birth."

Think about how far Naomi has come. In chapter one, she told these same women to call her "Mara" (Bitter) because "the

Almighty has made my life very bitter." She said she went away full but came back empty. She accused God of afflicting her and bringing misfortune on her.

Now? Now the women are praising God for his faithfulness. Now Naomi has a grandson who will provide for her in her old age. Now her emptiness has been filled to overflowing.

And did you catch that incredible statement about Ruth? "Your daughter-in-law, who loves you and who is better to you than seven sons." In a culture where sons were everything—where a woman's value was often measured by how many sons she produced—to say that Ruth was worth more than seven sons was the highest possible compliment. Ruth, the Moabite widow, had proven herself to be more valuable than the ideal family everyone dreamed of having.

Then Naomi took the child in her arms and cared for him. The women of the neighborhood said, "Naomi has a son!" and they named him Obed. The woman who called herself empty now held fullness in her arms.

THE SURPRISE ENDING

If the story ended here, it would be a beautiful conclusion. A widow finds love. A foreigner finds acceptance. A grieving mother-in-law finds joy again. The end.

But the narrator has one more surprise for us. "He was the father of Jesse, the father of David."

Wait—David? As in King David? The shepherd boy who killed Goliath? The greatest king in Israel's history? The man after God's own heart? The one whose throne God promised would last forever?

Yes. That David.

And just to make sure we understand the significance, the narrator adds a genealogy—a family tree stretching from Perez (Judah and Tamar's son) all the way down to David: Perez → Hezron → Ram → Amminadab → Nahshon → Salmon → Boaz → Obed → Jesse → David

Ten generations. And right there in the middle, in the honored seventh position, is Boaz—the man who chose to redeem a Moabite widow when no one else would.

This genealogy reveals that the book of Ruth was never just about Ruth, Naomi, and Boaz. It was always about God's bigger plan to bring salvation to the world. Through this unlikely family, God was building the royal line that would produce David.

And if you keep following that family tree forward? It leads to Jesus. Matthew's gospel begins with a genealogy that traces Jesus' ancestry all the way back through David to Abraham. And right there in Matthew 1:5, we read: "Salmon the father of Boaz, whose mother was Rahab, Boaz the father of Obed, whose mother was Ruth, Obed the father of Jesse, and Jesse the father of King David."

Ruth made it into the genealogy of Jesus. The Moabite widow. The foreigner. The outsider. She's listed among the ancestors of the Son of God.

WHAT THIS MEANS FOR US

So what does Ruth chapter four have to say to you?

First, your choices matter more than you know. Mr. So-and-So made a practical, self-protective decision—and he disappeared from history without a trace. Boaz made a sacrificial, others-focused decision—and he became an ancestor of the Messiah. Neither of them could see the long-term consequences of their choices. But their choices mattered.

The same is true for you. Every day, you make decisions that seem small and insignificant. Will you be kind to that kid everyone ignores? Will you tell the truth even when lying would be easier? Will you help someone even when there's nothing in it for you? Those choices might seem minor right now. But you never know how God might use them. Your faithfulness today could have ripple effects that last for generations.

Second, God's story is bigger than your story—and that's good news. Ruth was just trying to survive. She had no idea she was playing a role in God's cosmic plan of redemption. But she was. Her ordinary life was woven into an extraordinary story.

The same is true for you. Your life might feel ordinary. But if you belong to God, your story is part of HIS story—the story of how he is rescuing and redeeming a broken world through Jesus Christ. You matter. Your life matters. Not because you're famous or powerful, but because the God of the universe has chosen to include you in what he's doing.

Third, God welcomes outsiders. Ruth was a Moabite—a member of a nation that was excluded from Israel's assembly by law. She was a widow, a foreigner, a nobody. And yet God brought her into the very center of his plan. He didn't just tolerate her; he honored her. Her name is recorded in the genealogy of Jesus.

If you ever feel like an outsider—like you don't belong, like you're too messed up, like God could never use someone like you—Ruth's story says otherwise. God specializes in welcoming outsiders. He delights in using unlikely people to accomplish his purposes. You are not disqualified.

Fourth, faithful love (*hesed*) changes everything. The book of Ruth is saturated with *hesed*—that loyal, committed, self-sacrificing love that keeps showing up even when it's costly. Ruth showed *hesed* to Naomi. Boaz showed *hesed* to Ruth. And behind it all, God was showing *hesed* to everyone—faithfully working out his good purposes even when no one could see it.

That same *hesed* love is available to you through Jesus. He is the ultimate Redeemer—the one who paid the price to rescue you, not because you deserved it, but because he loves you. And as you receive that love, you're empowered to show it to others.

Fifth, empty can become full. Naomi's story arc is one of the most powerful parts of this book. She started full and ended up empty. She was bitter, hopeless, and convinced that God was against her. But she was wrong. God wasn't against her—he was working for her good the entire time. By the end of the story, her arms were full, her heart was full, and her life was overflowing with blessing.

If you're going through a hard time right now—if you feel empty, forgotten, or abandoned—Naomi's story is for you. Your emptiness is not the end of your story. The God who filled Naomi's arms with Obed is the same God who is working in your life right now. Hold on. Keep trusting. Fullness is coming.

TALKING POINTS

Here are some things to think about and discuss:

1. **Mr. So-and-So prioritized protecting his own stuff over helping his family.** What are some ways we can fall into

the same trap—choosing self-interest over helping others?

2. **Boaz made a costly choice that ended up having consequences he never imagined.** Can you think of a time when a small act of kindness or faithfulness led to something bigger than you expected?

3. **Ruth is listed in the genealogy of Jesus.** What does it mean to you that God includes unlikely people—foreigners, outsiders, people with messy backgrounds—in his story?

4. **Naomi went from "empty" to "full" by the end of the book.** How does her story give you hope when you're going through difficult times?

5. **The book of Ruth shows ordinary people living faithful lives without knowing how their choices fit into God's bigger plan.** How does that change the way you think about your own ordinary, everyday decisions?

The story of Ruth ends with a baby in Naomi's arms and a genealogy that stretches into the future. But in another sense, it doesn't really end at all. The story continues through Obed, through Jesse, through David, through generation after generation—until finally, in a stable in Bethlehem (the same town where Ruth gleaned barley!), a baby was born who would be called Jesus.

Ruth's story became part of Jesus' story. And if you trust in him, your story becomes part of his story too.

That's the beautiful truth of the book of Ruth: God is always working, always weaving, always bringing his good purposes to completion. Even when you can't see it. Even when you feel empty. Even when life doesn't make sense.

CONCLUSION: THE ROAD GOES EVER ON

Remember where this story started?

A family fleeing a famine. A woman burying her husband. Then burying her sons. A bitter widow walking home with nothing but grief and a stubborn daughter-in-law who refused to leave her side.

It looked like the end. It felt like the end. Naomi was so convinced it was the end that she told everyone to call her "Bitter."

But it wasn't the end. It was actually a beginning.

Ruth gleaned in a field. Boaz noticed her. A late-night conversation led to a wedding. A wedding led to a baby. And that baby—little Obed, bouncing on Naomi's lap while the neighborhood women smiled and praised God—that baby was just the start of something nobody could have imagined.

Obed grew up and had a son named Jesse. Jesse had a son named David—the shepherd boy who killed a giant, wrote psalms, and became the greatest king Israel ever knew. And if you follow David's family tree down through the centuries, through good kings and bad kings, through exile and return, through four hundred years of silence... you eventually arrive at another baby born in Bethlehem.

His name was Jesus.

More than a thousand years after Ruth arrived in Bethlehem as a poor foreigner, a carpenter named Joseph made the same journey. He was traveling from Nazareth to Bethlehem because the Roman emperor had ordered everyone to return to their hometown to be counted. Joseph went to Bethlehem because he belonged to the family line of David—which means he was also part of the family line of Ruth and Boaz.

While Joseph was there, his wife Mary gave birth to a baby boy. They wrapped him in cloths and laid him in a manger because there was no room for them anywhere else.

That baby, a descendant of Ruth the Moabite and Boaz the redeemer, grew up to become the Savior of the world.

Think about that for a second. When Ruth was trudging down the road to Bethlehem, exhausted and hungry and scared about the future, she had no idea that her great-great-great-(lots more greats)-grandson would be born in that same little town. She had no idea that her story would be remembered and retold for thousands of years. She had no idea that her act of *hesed*—her stubborn, loyal love for Naomi—was part of God's plan to rescue the entire human race.

Ruth couldn't see any of that. She was just trying to survive.

But God saw it. God was weaving her story into something so much bigger than she could imagine.

Here's what I want you to take away from this book: your story matters more than you know.

Right now, you might feel like Ruth felt on that road to

Bethlehem—tired, confused, uncertain about the future. Maybe you're going through something hard. Maybe life hasn't turned out the way you expected. Maybe you're wondering if God even notices you at all.

He does. He notices. And he's working.

The same God who guided Ruth's steps to Boaz's field is guiding your steps too. The same God who brought blessing out of Naomi's bitterness is working in your life right now—even if you can't see it, even if you can't feel it.

That's what the book of Ruth teaches us. God doesn't abandon us when life falls apart. He doesn't forget us when we're struggling. He's always working beneath the surface, moving pieces into place, writing a story that's bigger than we can imagine.

But there's one more part of the story we need to talk about.

Jesus didn't just come to be born in Bethlehem. He came to walk his own hard road—a road that led from Jerusalem to a hill called Golgotha, where he was nailed to a cross.

If Ruth's road was difficult, Jesus' road was the hardest anyone has ever walked. He was rejected, beaten, mocked, and killed—even though he had never done anything wrong. It was the darkest day in human history.

And yet... God was working even then.

The Bible tells us that Jesus' death wasn't an accident. It wasn't a tragedy that caught God off guard. It was part of God's plan all along—a plan to rescue people who couldn't rescue themselves. Just like Boaz redeemed Ruth, paying the price to make her part of his family, Jesus redeemed us, paying the ultimate price to make us part of God's family.

What Boaz was to Ruth, Jesus is to us.

We were outsiders, foreigners, people with no claim to God's kindness. But Jesus—our true *go'el*, our Redeemer—spread the corner of his garment over us. He sheltered us under his wings. He paid a price we could never pay so that we could belong to him forever.

And here's the amazing part: if God could take the worst day in history and turn it into the salvation of the world, then there's nothing in your life that he can't redeem. No mistake is too big. No situation is too hopeless. No road is too dark.

God specializes in bringing good out of bad, hope out of despair, life out of death. That's what he does. That's who he is.

So what do you do with all of this?

First, trust God even when you can't see what he's doing. Ruth had no idea where her story was going. Neither did Naomi. Neither did Boaz. They just took the next faithful step and trusted God with the rest. You can do the same thing. You don't have to understand God's whole plan—you just have to trust that he has one.

Second, show *hesed* to the people around you. Be the kind of friend who doesn't walk away when things get hard. Be the kind of person who notices people who are struggling and goes out of your way to help them. Be a Ruth to someone who needs loyalty. Be a Boaz to someone who needs kindness. You never know how God might use your small act of faithfulness to change someone's life—or even change history.

Third, remember that your story isn't over yet. If this were chapter one of Ruth, you'd think the story was hopeless. But chapter one isn't the end. Neither is whatever chapter you're living through right now. God is still writing. The best part might still be ahead.

The road to Bethlehem wasn't easy for Ruth. It won't always be easy for you either. Life is hard sometimes. People let us down. Things don't go the way we planned. We face loss and disappointment and pain.

But we don't walk alone.

We have a God who sees us, who loves us, who is working all things together for good. We have a Redeemer who paid the ultimate price to call us his own. And we have the promise that no matter how dark the road gets, the harvest is coming.

Naomi learned that lesson. So did Ruth. And so can you.

Whatever road you're walking right now, keep going. Keep trusting. Keep showing *hesed*. Keep your eyes open for the ways God is working—because he is, even when you can't see it.

The God of Ruth is your God too.

And he's not finished with your story yet.

www.ingramcontent.com/pod-product-compliance
Ingram Content Group UK Ltd.
Pitfield, Milton Keynes, MK11 3LW, UK
UKHW020420250726
13967UKWH00007B/2746